Animal Habitats

The Man-of-War at Sea

**Text by
Jennifer Coldrey
and David Shale**

**Photographs by
Oxford Scientific Films**

Methuen Children's Books
in association with Belitha Press

The Portuguese Man-of-War floats at the surface of the sea, where its blue colours blend in well with its surroundings.

A living Man-of-War and where to find it

The surface of the sea is a big, wide open *habitat*. In *tropical* waters the surface is frequently dotted with small objects that look like inflated blue plastic bags. Each 'bag' is the float of one of the most extraordinary of all sea creatures, a kind of jellyfish called the Portuguese Man-of-War. English sailors in the 1400s first gave it that name because it looked like a caravel, the small handy ship in which Portuguese sailors explored the seas. The caravel had a triangular, fore-and-aft sail, called a 'lateen sail'. This sail was developed by Arab sailors in the Mediterranean Sea.

The Portuguese Man-of-War also has a sail, a sort of crest that lies fore-and-aft on top of the float. This float allows it to sail with the wind like a tiny boat.

The Portuguese Man-of-War is found in warm seas all over the world. It lives among the *plankton*, the mass of small plants and animals that floats in the upper waters of the oceans. It is much bigger than most other plankton animals, but, like the rest of the plankton, it drifts with the ocean waves. Now and again winds or strong currents catch Men-of-War and

A Portuguese caravel, showing the lateen sail.

drive them towards land, where their bodies are washed up on the beach. Groups of several thousand may be found together. Sometimes a few are carried to the cooler waters of Europe where they can be seen lying on the sands.

As their bodies dry out in the sun, their floats slowly collapse and the tentacles shrivel. Their stranded bodies are easy to see as they lie on the beach, and many animals, including crabs, come to feed on them.

Out at sea a Portuguese Man-of-War is much harder to spot because its blue colouring *camouflages* it well in the water. In sunlight, the float is a bright, shimmering blue, but in dull light it may appear greenish. These colours make the animal fairly hard to pick out against the shifting surface of the sea.

This Portuguese Man-of-War has just been stranded on a beach in Bermuda. Its float and crest are still full of air.

What sort of animal is the Portuguese Man-of-War?

The Portuguese Man-of-War is related to true jellyfish and other sea jellies. It is a member of a large group of water animals known as *coelenterates,* a Latin-based word that means 'hollow guts'. The shape and size of coelenterates varies a great deal but, basically, each animal is a living, flexible, jelly-like bag – a hollow gut – with a mouth at one end. There is no opening at the other end of the body, so food remains pass out of the mouth. Tentacles surround the mouth and push food into it. The simplest type of coelenterate is called a *polyp,* of which the sea anemone is a good example. The Portuguese Man-of-War is a more complicated type.

Some coelenterates, including the sea anemones, live attached to weeds or to the bottom of the sea. Others, including the true jellyfish and the Portuguese Man-of-War, float freely in the water. All coelenterates have stinging cells or *nematocysts*.

Like other coelenterates, the Portuguese Man-of-War is a very primitive animal. It has no skeleton and no obvious head or tail. It has no brain, but only a very simple nervous system, and no heart or blood vessels to carry food and oxygen around the body. Coelenterates breathe by simply absorbing oxygen from the surrounding water into their bodies. They do not have gills for breathing like crabs and fishes do.

The Portuguese Man-of-War is an unusual kind of sea jelly. All we see of it, above the surface, is the bottle-like float with its wavy crest. However, just as we see only a small part of an iceberg, so the main part of the animal is hidden beneath the waves. Underneath, the Man-of-War looks like an upside-down bush. It has long tentacles which trail away in the water. These tentacles act as a living fishing net for catching food.

However, this is no ordinary fishing net. The tentacles are armed with millions of nematocysts which paralyse or kill *prey*. They make this animal greatly feared by bathers, for the stings can be very painful and may even make a person ill for several days. Fortunately, people do not often come into contact with Portuguese Men-of-War, because these animals normally live far out at sea.

Beneath the surface, the Portuguese Man-of-War has long, stinging tentacles which trail away into the waters below.

Many tentacles and other persons hang beneath the float of a Portuguese Man-of-War.

The floating commune

The most remarkable thing about the Portuguese Man-of-War is that it is not simply one animal like most other sea jellies. It is a floating commune, a colony of individual polyps which zoologists commonly refer to as 'persons'. A fully-grown Man-of-War may have as many as a thousand persons. All the persons are closely linked and dependent upon each other so that they all act together as if they were a single animal.

The Portuguese Man-of-War consists of four different kinds of person. The float is the first kind. It is a long, gas-filled bladder like a miniature balloon. Set diagonally along the top of this bladder is the thin, wavy crest, often tinged mauve or pink. The float varies from the size of a pea when the animal is very young to about 12 in (300 mm) long when it is fully grown. Its top may rise as much as 6 in (150 mm) above the surface of the water. Its function is to keep the Man-of-War bobbing along on the surface of the sea, while the crest acts as a sail. The float is an overgrown polyp, which has formed into a closed bag. The other members of the colony grow from it and hang down into the water below.

The tentacles are a second kind of person. Some are much larger than others. When fully extended the long tentacles can be as thin as a human hair. They vary in length from 10 to 100 ft (3-30 m). When these long tentacles are not extended for fishing they can be drawn up into concertina-like coils. The Portuguese Man-of-War uses them to haul up food to its many mouths. A fully-grown Man-of-War has seven or more large tentacles and many smaller ones. The tentacles are useful weapons of defence as well as a means of catching food. Along their length are thousands of nematocysts.

The stinging tentacles hang down in the water like a curtain of beads.

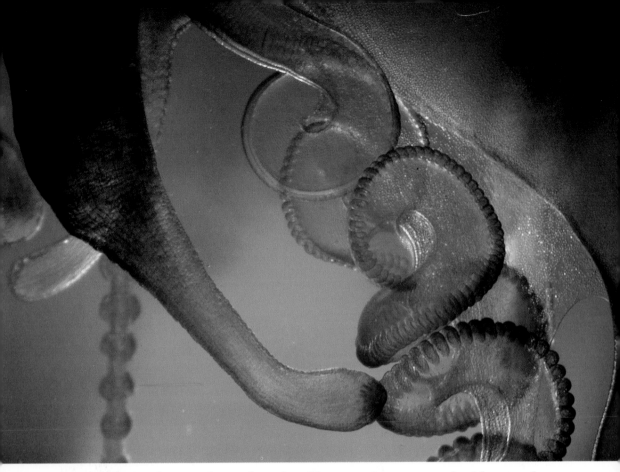

Among the tentacles are long, bag-like stomach persons, each with a mouth at one end.

More persons in the commune

The third kind of persons are called *gasterozooids*, or stomach-persons. They digest the prey caught by the tentacles. Instead of having just one stomach, the Man-of-War has many. Each stomach-person is a kind of polyp, a long bag with a narrow mouth at one end. However, unlike a true polyp, there are no tentacles around the mouth.

The fourth kind of persons are *gonozooids*, which are the sex organs or reproductive parts of the animal. They hang down among the tentacles like bunches of pink mistletoe. A Portuguese Man-of-War is either male or female. Males have sex organs that produce sperms, while females produce eggs. No one knows quite how these animals reproduce but biologists have found baby Portuguese Men-of-War in the sea, each consisting of just a tiny float with a single tentacle hanging down. They assume that these young polyps grew from fertilised eggs that their parents shed into the sea.

The large pink cluster is one of the reproductive persons of the Portuguese Man-of-War.

The baby polyp and its float form the basis for the whole colony. As the float grows, other small polyps develop from it until a complete Man-of-War is formed. The smallest specimens of Men-of-War that have been found are less than 1/10 in (2 mm) long. These are very young animals indeed. In about a month they grow to 1 in (25 mm) or more in length. It takes several months for a complete animal to develop. As the Portuguese Man-of-War grows older, it adds more persons to its colony. It never really stops growing, although no specimens bigger than about 12 in (300 mm) across have been found.

Here you can see the difference between a very young and a much older Portuguese Man-of-War. The baby animal is about 2 in (5 cm) long.

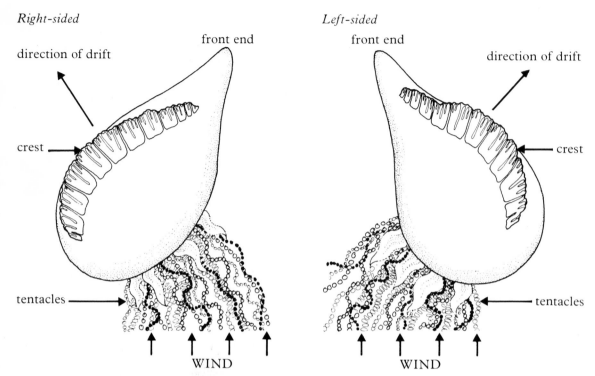

Right-sided

direction of drift

front end

crest

tentacles

WIND

Left-sided

front end

direction of drift

crest

tentacles

WIND

The difference between a left-sided and a right-sided Portuguese Man-of-War.

Floating and sailing with the wind

A Portuguese Man-of-War cannot swim. It simply drifts and floats wherever the current and the wind take it. The float keeps it from sinking, while the crest acts like a sail, catching the wind and driving the animal along. The Man-of-War has no control over where it goes, nor over the speed at which it travels. When the wind blows at an angle to the sail, it can drive the animal along at a speed of just over 1 mph (almost 2 km/h).

Now and again the animal seems to change shape as its crest becomes more or less inflated with air. A *gland* at the base of the float keeps the gas mixture topped up. The amount of air in the sail controls the extent to which it is affected by the wind.

From time to time the float flops over and dips in the water, but the animal pulls itself upright a few minutes later by contracting the muscles in the wall of the float. This tilting over seems to occur mainly in calm weather, and helps to keep the float moist. In rough weather the animal stays upright, and spray from the sea wets the float.

The Portuguese Man-of-War is not symmetrical like a sailing ship. Underneath it is lop-sided, with most of its tentacles and other persons hanging down from a bulge on one side of the body, generally the *wind-ward* side.

Some Portuguese Men-of-War are right-sided and some are left-sided. This affects the way in which they are driven by the wind – a left-sided Man-of-War drifts at an angle of 45 degrees to the right of the direction from which the wind is blowing, while a right-sided animal drifts 45 degrees to the left. The two kinds of the Portuguese Man-of-War are mirror images of one another, and so they move in opposite directions in response to the wind. This variation helps to distribute the animals more evenly over the warm oceans of the world.

A Portuguese Man-of-War tilts over to wet its float and crest in the water.

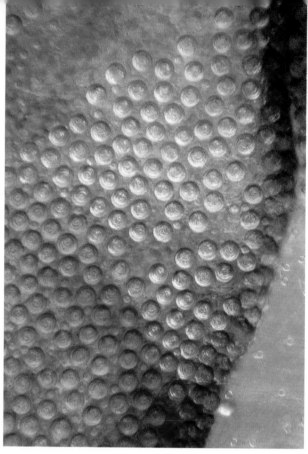

Each tentacle is armed, from end to end, with thousands of stinging cells (nematocysts) arranged in bands.

In this close-up picture, you can just see how the stinging threads are coiled up inside each cell before they are fired.

Poisonous tentacles

From above the surface of the sea the Portuguese Man-of-War looks a fairly harmless creature. But to unwary fish in the water below, it is a dangerous *predator* and about as deadly as a cobra. Like other jellyfish, its tentacles are armed with rows of stinging cells containing a powerful poison.

Each stinging cell, or nematocyst, is in effect like a miniature hypodermic syringe. If a fish or other animal touches a tentacle, the stinging cells nearby are triggered into action. Each cell shoots out a hollow thread with a needle-sharp tip, rather like a harpoon on the end of a line. Before being used, the stinging thread is stored inside its cell like the tucked-in finger of a rubber glove.

When the cell fires, the thread is exploded outwards – just like that pushed-in rubber glove finger if you blow hard into it. At the base of each stinging thread are several barbs, or hooks, which grip the victim. As the prey is pierced, the poison shoots down the thread and into the victim's body. The poison acts quickly enough to paralyse a fish in a few seconds.

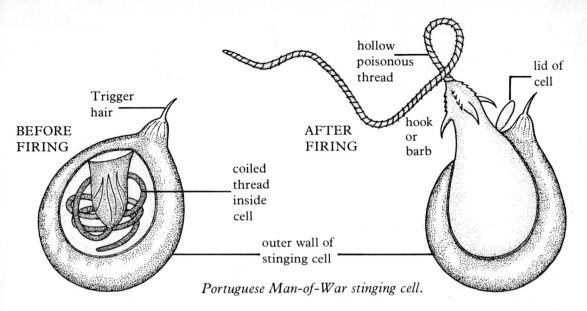

BEFORE FIRING

Trigger hair

AFTER FIRING

hollow poisonous thread

lid of cell

hook or barb

coiled thread inside cell

outer wall of stinging cell

Portuguese Man-of-War stinging cell.

Humans swimming in the sea can be badly stung, too. On some tropical beaches warning notices are put up when there are Portuguese Men-of-War about, and people in these places are advised not to go in the water. The immediate effect of brushing against a tentacle is a violent burning or stinging sensation. If you are stung on the hand or arm the pain gradually creeps up the arm to the armpit. A sting on the foot sends the pain up to the groin. A slight sting is painful, but it disappears after some hours. People with severe stings often suffer from shock and have been known to collapse unconscious. A bad sting leaves an angry, red weal which lasts several weeks.

Now they have exploded! Something has touched the tentacle and the nearby stinging threads have shot out to inject their poison.

This Portuguese Man-of-War has captured many fish. Each one is being eaten by a different stomach.

Catching food

As the Portuguese Man-of-War drifts through the sea, its lethal curtain of tentacles streams behind it to trap unwary victims. When a fish or other creature comes into contact with one of the tentacles it is hooked and poisoned, all at once. The tentacle then hauls up the prey to the stomach-persons. A fully-extended tentacle may be up to 70 times as long as one that is coiled up. Each tentacle works independently. While one is hauling in its catch, the others remain streaming in the water, ready to catch more prey.

Any stomach-persons near the captured prey begin to twist about when they sense the approaching food, as if searching for it. When they find the prey their mouths open to engulf it. The mouth is only about 1/25 in (1 mm) across when resting, but it can stretch to more than $\frac{3}{4}$ in (20 mm) across when feeding. The Portuguese Man-of-War feeds mainly on fish fry (young fish), as well as shrimps and other small animals in the plankton. These animals, no more than 1-2 in (25-50 mm) across, are small enough to make a single mouthful.

Sometimes the Portuguese Man-of-War traps and consumes quite large fishes, such as flying fish and mackerel, though fish as large as this generally manage to escape. To deal with such a big meal, several stomach-persons usually fasten their mouths like suckers on to the fish until its whole body is completely covered. Each stomach releases a supply of digestive juice which breaks down and absorbs a part of the fish. In this way several stomach-persons get a share of one fish.

The food of the Portuguese Man-of-War is digested in the bag-like stomachs and, in due course, any indigestible remains are pushed out through the mouths. The nourishment from the digested food is absorbed into the body and eventually circulates to all the different persons in the colony.

A Portuguese Man-of-War can usually find plenty of food in the sea as it sails through the water. However, the best feeding time is at night when many animals move up from below towards the surface of the ocean.

When a large fish like this is caught, the mouths of many stomach persons move down to engulf the prey.

The Ocean Sunfish sometimes feeds on Portuguese Men-of-War when it swims near the surface.

Large enemies of the Portuguese Man-of-War

You might think that a creature as poisonous and deadly as the Portuguese Man-of-War would be safe from predators. Yet it too has its enemies, which seem to be unaffected by its venom.

The largest of these enemies is the Ocean Sunfish, the biggest of the bony fishes. This giant fish weighs about 1100 lb (500 kg) and may be as much as 10 ft (3 m) long. It is an oval-shaped fish which is occasionally seen swimming so close to the surface that its dorsal or rear fin appears above the water. In deeper water the Sunfish eats various sea jellies and young fish. When near the surface, it occasionally eats living Men-of-War, either whole or piece by piece, and seems none the worse for its strange diet.

When at sea, a Loggerhead Turtle will happily eat its way through a Portuguese Man-of-War.

Two sea turtles, the Loggerhead and Hawksbill, are also known to eat Portuguese Men-of-War. The Loggerhead Turtle has been seen munching its way through this menacing meal with its eyes shut to keep out the stings, trailing tentacles from its jaws like a messy feeder with spaghetti.

In the Mediterranean Sea there is an octopus which is not afraid of the Portuguese Man-of-War's poison, but uses it as a hunting weapon. It breaks off lengths of tentacles which it grasps in its suckers to stun and kill its own prey.

Human beings, although not predators, can also be enemies of the Man-of-War. People pollute the ocean and harm its wildlife with poisonous chemicals from industry and agriculture. Oil pollution can kill Portuguese Men-of-War, along with other surface life, when large amounts of oil are spilled and slicks spread over the sea.

A Sally Lightfoot Crab feeds on a Portuguese Man-of-War washed ashore on a beach in Bermuda.

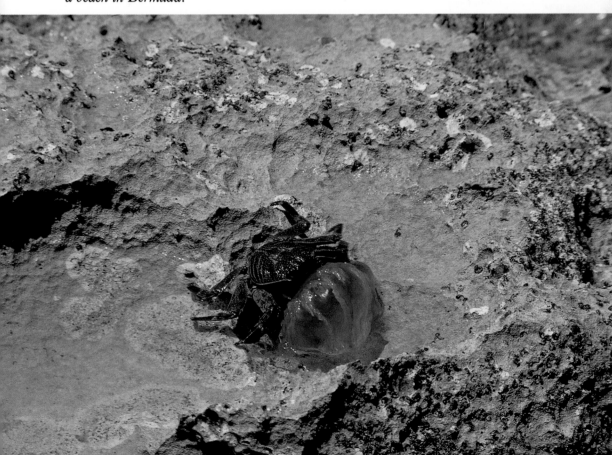

A Violet Sea Snail feeds hungrily on the body of a Portuguese Man-of-War.

Small enemies of the Portuguese Man-of-War

A smaller enemy is the Violet Sea Snail. The shell of this animal, which is just over $\frac{5}{8}$ in (15 mm) long, is a delicate violet in colour. It lives at the surface of the sea, hanging literally for dear life from a raft of air bubbles. If it let go it would sink to the bottom of the sea. The Violet Sea Snail makes the bubbles by trapping air from above the surface in a slimy *mucus* which it produces from its foot. The mucus hardens when it comes into contact with the air. This colourful sea snail feeds on the Man-of-War by rasping away with its rough tongue, apparently not suffering from the effects of the stinging tentacles.

Another small enemy of the Portuguese Man-of-War is a cousin of the sea snail, the sea slug *Glaucus*. This slug lives upside down just under the surface of the water, and is kept afloat by a bubble of air in its stomach. *Glaucus* eats any part of the Man-of-War that it can reach, including the stinging cells. It absorbs the unexploded stinging cells into its digestive system without setting them off, and uses them later, as second-hand weapons, to fight off any sea animal that attacks it.

Wind and waves are responsible for the death of many Portuguese Men-of-War. From time to time these creatures are washed up in their thousands on beaches, particularly after storms. Long after the gas-filled floats have collapsed and withered in the sun, the stinging cells remain active, still able to cause serious pain to anyone who steps on or touches them. Yet a dead Man-of-War is still a welcome food for some animals, including many crabs, which feed untroubled on the bodies as they lie dead on the sand.

Here the sea slug, Glaucus, *with its feathery limbs, nibbles at the tentacles of a Portuguese Man-of-War.*

Three mottled clownfish swim along boldly among the tentacles of a Portuguese Man-of-War, without fear of being stung.

The friendly clownfish

Although the Portuguese Man-of-War is avoided by most of his fellow sea creatures, there is one fish that regards it as a friend. This is a little clownfish, which is often called the Man-of-War Fish because of its association with its deadly companion. It lives quite happily among the tentacles of the Man-of-War, and is rarely seen anywhere else. The clown-fish is about 3 in (75 mm) long, much smaller than a fully-grown Man-of-War. It has a silvery body marked with streaks and blotches of dark blue, which make it difficult to see among the Portuguese Man-of-War's tentacles.

As the clownfish swims in and out through the trailing tentacles it frequently brushes against them, but is never stung. It appears that the fish produces a slimy mucus which causes the Portuguese Man-of-War to hold its fire. However, if the fish becomes injured it loses its immunity, and ends up as the host's next meal!

The clownfish seems to receive all the benefits in its strange partnership with the Portuguese Man-of-War. The main benefit is the protection it receives against enemies such as large, hungry fish. If danger threatens, the clownfish hides close up under the Man-of-War's float where it is safely out of reach behind the curtain of tentacles. The clownfish may also gain by eating some of the Man-of-War's leftovers, and it is even said to nibble at the tentacles themselves from time to time.

Other fishes have occasionally been seen living in company with the Portuguese Man-of-War. One of them, called a yellow-jack, does so only when it is young and small.

Many relatives of the Portuguese Man-of-War, including jellyfish and sea anemones, are known to have fishes living among their tentacles. Hermit crabs, which live in the discarded shells of whelks and other sea snails, put sea anemones on top of their shells for protection, and the sea anemones live on scraps of the crabs' food. This kind of partnership, in which both parties benefit, is called *symbiosis*. A one-sided arrangement, such as the clownfish and the Portuguese Man-of-War have, is known as *commensalism*.

Other kinds of clownfish live happily among the stinging tentacles of large sea anemones.

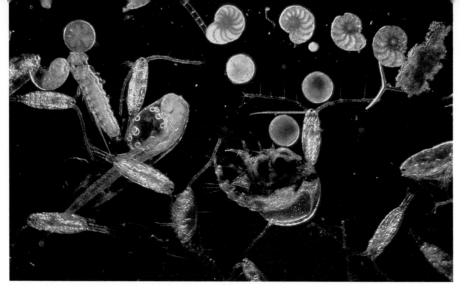

Under a microscope, this drop of sea-water is seen to contain many tiny animals and plants, including small shrimps, shells, a baby crab and a fish larva.

The world of plankton

On land, all life begins with plants. They can build themselves from simple chemicals, drawn from the soil and the air. They use power from the sun to make their food, in a process known as *photosynthesis*. Life in the sea also begins with plants, but we cannot see most of them because they are so small. They are like a fine dust, drifting in the upper layers of the sea. These tiny floating plants can only flourish at depths where the light of the sun can reach them. These depths vary – in clear water the light may penetrate as far down as 300 ft (100 m). If you look at a drop of sea water under the microscope, you can see that there must be billions of these tiny plants in the ocean.

Large shoals of fish fry swarm near the surface of the sea and make up part of the plankton.

The tiny animals that float among the microscopic plants and feed on them are also numbered in billions. The largest are about the size of a grain of rice, and the smallest only the size of a pin's head. They include shrimp-like creatures, worms, tiny snails and jellyfish, and also the eggs and *larvae* of young fish. All these tiny plants and animals are collectively known as plankton, from a Greek word meaning 'drifters'. Biologists call the plants phytoplankton and the animals zooplankton, from two other Greek words meaning 'plant' and 'animal' respectively.

Unlike the phytoplankton, the animals of the zooplankton do not rely on sunlight to help them get their food, so they do not have to stay close to the surface of the sea. Most of them swim near the surface at night to feed on the plants, but before dawn they sink down to deeper water where it is cooler and the light is less bright. In the depths of the sea the currents move at speeds different from those on the surface. They carry the zoo-plankton with them, and move them horizontally. So when the animals next rise up to feed, they find themselves in 'fresh pastures'.

The Portuguese Man-of-War is one of several larger animals that are included among the plankton. They, too, float and drift near the surface and make the most of the rich supplies of food found in the plankton 'soup'.

Some of the plankton animals float at the surface. Here is a young Portuguese Man-of-War surrounded by two white shells, and some sea jellies called Porpita.

More floating jellies

There are many types of sea jellies that float either at the surface of the sea or just below it. One sea jelly, which has habits rather like those of the Portuguese Man-of-War, has the romantic names of Jack Sail-by-the-Wind, or By-the-Wind Sailor. These names were given to the animal by the 'old salts' of sailing-ship days, who used to see fleets of these little craft bobbing along on the waves.

Jack Sail-by-the-Wind is smaller than a Portuguese Man-of-War. Its horny float consists of an oval raft about 1 in by 1½ in (25 mm by 40 mm) with a triangular sail set at an angle across it. The float consists of a series of air-filled chambers, a small one in the centre and the others in a series of rings around it. As the animal grows bigger it adds extra buoyancy rings to its float.

Like the Man-of-War, Jack Sail-by-the-Wind has a number of persons hanging under the float. There is one central stomach-person with a big mouth. This is surrounded by reproductive persons (gonozooids), while around these there is a ring of short tentacles armed with stinging-cells. The poison is much less powerful than that of the Man-of-War. The whole animal, including its sail, is blue, tinged with purple.

As it sails along on the surface, Jack Sail-by-the-Wind feeds on tiny plants and animals in the plankton, which it catches with its stinging tentacles.

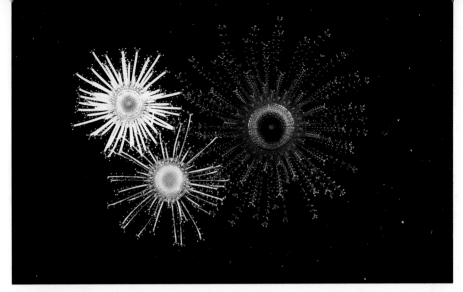

Seen from above, a group of Porpitas *look like a miniature set of star-burst Christmas decorations.*

Jack Sail-by-the-Wind has another likeness to the Man-of-War: there are two kinds, right-handed and left-handed. They cruise the wide oceans in huge armadas, sometimes thousands upon thousands of them, spread out on the water as far as the eye can see.

Another tiny sea jelly found floating on the ocean surface is *Porpita*, which has no popular name. It has a circular float but no sail, and is only about 1 in (25 mm) across. Underneath, there is a central mouth surrounded by reproductive bodies. Stiff, knobbly tentacles stick out from the edge of the float, like the spokes on a wheel. *Porpitas* are usually blue, but other colours have been seen, including bright yellow and brown. The animals are often found in shoals in the warm waters of the Mediterranean Sea and the North Atlantic Ocean.

This is what Porpita *looks like below the surface. The stinging cells are arranged in knobs on the tentacles.*

This Lion's Mane Jellyfish from Australian waters has a thick mass of tentacles. A shoal of fish shelter beneath it as it swims along.

Swimming jellies

Many other types of jellyfish live in the sea, and some occasionally come into contact with the Portuguese Man-of-War. The true jellyfishes swim or float in the waters below the surface. Although they spend part of their time floating, they are active swimmers and so, unlike the Portuguese Man-of-War, they do not have to depend on wind and waves to move them about. Jellyfishes come in all shapes and sizes. Some are as small as a pea, others can be larger than a dinner-plate. The giant jellyfish *Cyanea* that lives in the Arctic Ocean can be more than 7 ft (2 m) across.

A true jellyfish has a body shaped like a bell or an umbrella. It swims by opening and closing its umbrella, forcing the water out behind and driving itself along by jet propulsion. The mouth with its long neck hangs in the middle like the handle of the umbrella, and there is a fringe of tentacles around the edge. The number and type of tentacles varies from animal to animal. In some jellyfish the mouth is drawn out to form long frilly 'arms', which sting and catch food like tentacles.

Like the Portuguese Man-of-War the true jellyfish have nematocysts on their tentacles with which they sting and catch their prey. Unlike the Portuguese Man-of-War, however, a true jellyfish is not made up of a group of polyps but is one single person.

The comb jellies are another group of sea jellies which are often found in surface waters. They have delicate transparent bodies, shaped like tiny eggs or footballs. On the outside of their bodies are eight rows of comb-like plates, which beat to and fro to make the animal move through the water. As the hair-like combs vibrate you can see waves of rainbow colours move along them, although the bodies of the animals are almost invisible in the water. All comb jellies are *luminescent* – they glow at night with a greenish-blue light.

Comb jellies do not have stinging cells. Instead they are armed with sticky cells which catch prey like underwater flypapers. The smallest comb jellies are pea-sized. The sea gooseberries, which are among the best known, are about $\frac{3}{4}$ in (20 mm) long. They each have two long, branched, sticky tentacles which they use to snare their prey.

A comb jelly glows with rainbow colours as its comb-plates beat to and fro to propel it through the water.

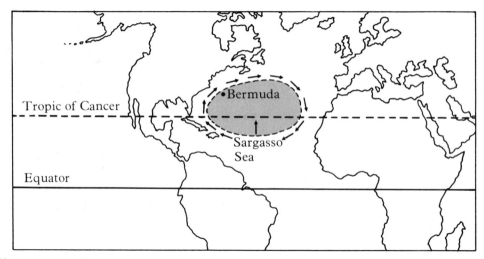

The seaweed sea

One place where you can find the Portuguese Man-of-War is the Sargasso Sea. The Sargasso is a part of the Atlantic Ocean lying to the east of North America and north of the West Indies. It was first sighted by Christopher Columbus in 1492 and covers an area about half the size of Europe. The Sargasso Sea has no land boundaries, but swift ocean currents, including the Gulf Stream, surround it. Inside the loop of these currents is an area of calm, slow-moving water. The movement of the currents around it, aided by the rotation of the Earth, causes the water to pile up towards the centre of the Sargasso Sea. The sea-level there is about 3 ft (1 m) higher than in the surrounding ocean.

A large patch of Sargassum Weed floats on the surface of the Sargasso Sea.

At the surface of the Sargasso Sea floats seaweed – masses of it, in huge mats, some of them up to 100 ft (30 m) across. This is Sargassum Weed. The name Sargasso comes from the Portuguese word *sargaço*, a grape, because there are grape-like floats on the weed. Scientists think that Sargassum was originally a shore-based weed that drifted out to sea, where it grew successfully as a floating plant.

Most of the life in the Sargasso Sea is found among the Sargassum Weed. Here there are special animals that have adapted to life among the gold and olive-green fronds. Attached to the weed are sea anemones, sponges, stalked polyps, and tiny moss-animals. Sargassum rafts are also a base for small crabs, shrimps, sea-slugs and various fishes. The weed provides a vast pasture and shelter for these animals. Because the Sargasso Sea is relatively calm, the weed can float without being pounded to bits by storm-driven waves and the animals are protected too.

The currents swirling around the Sargasso Sea send drifting animals, including the Portuguese Man-of-War, to float among the rafts of sea-weed. Many other sea jellies are also found there. When a Portuguese Man-of-War blunders into a patch of Sargassum it is bound to find a rich supply of food. But it is also likely to become entangled among the fronds, where it is an easy prey for its own enemies such as *Glaucus,* the Violet Sea Snail, and the various crabs that live among the weed.

Among the Sargassum Weed hides a tiny crab. Crabs living in the weed would almost certainly attack any Portuguese Man-of-War that became entangled there.

Life on the ocean surface

To the casual eye the sea may look much the same everywhere, but even the surface varies in different parts of the world. Some regions are rich in the plant and animal life of the plankton, while others have much less. These areas of plenty and scarcity change daily, as the ocean currents move.

This ever-changing surface layer of the ocean is home for the Portuguese Man-of-War. Its way of life enables it to drift across the ocean, picking up food as it goes. It cannot hunt actively, but its trailing tentacles can net more than enough fish and other small sea creatures to keep it well supplied. Other animals feed on it, and so it forms part of a large food chain, in which the food and energy from plants is passed on through animals. We can show how that food chain works by drawing a diagram. As you can see, some pathways in the chain are more complicated than others.

Food chain

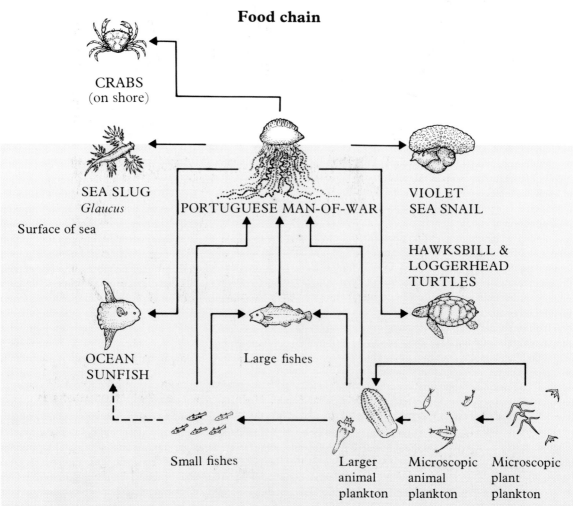

CRABS
(on shore)

SEA SLUG
Glaucus

Surface of sea

PORTUGUESE MAN-OF-WAR

VIOLET
SEA SNAIL

HAWKSBILL &
LOGGERHEAD
TURTLES

OCEAN
SUNFISH

Large fishes

Small fishes

Larger
animal
plankton

Microscopic
animal
plankton

Microscopic
plant
plankton

A Portuguese Man-of-War seen from below, its tentacles fishing the deep waters.

The Portuguese Man-of-War is well adapted to its life in this tossing, windswept habitat. Its float keeps it on the surface in spite of the buffeting by wind and waves, even in the worst storms. Its armoury of weapons is valuable for two reasons: to catch food and to ward off attacks by predators. Compared with other sea creatures, the Man-of-War has remarkably few enemies that can do it any harm. Provided it is not washed up on land by winds and tides, it is likely to survive for quite a long time in its wandering life in the open sea.

Glossary

camouflage :   the way an animal is disguised by blending in with its surroundings

coelenterates :   a group of jelly-like animals, including sea-anemones, corals and jellyfish

commensalism :   an association of two animals from which only one benefits

gasterozooids :   feeding polyps or 'stomach-persons'

gland :   an organ of the body that makes and secretes essential substances

gonozooids :   reproductive polyps bearing male or female sex organs

habitat :   the natural home of any plant or animal

larva   (plural *larvae*): young stage (after the egg) of many water animals

luminescent :   giving off light without heat

mucus :   slimy substance produced by some animals

nematocyst :   the stinging cell of a coelenterate

photosynthesis :   the process by which plants make their food, using energy from sunlight

plankton :   the mass of tiny plants and animals that drifts in the upper waters of the sea

polyp :   a simple, cylinder-shaped animal with a mouth at one end – the simplest form of coelenterate

predator :   an animal that kills and eats other animals

prey :   an animal that is killed and eaten by another animal

symbiosis :   a close association of two animals that depend on each other

tropical :   relating to the warm regions of the Earth lying either side of the Equator

windward :   side on which the wind blows

First published in Great Britain 1987
by Methuen Children's Books Ltd
11 New Fetter Lane, London EC4P 4EE
Conceived, designed and produced by Belitha Press Ltd
31 Newington Green, London N16 9PU
Copyright © in this format Belitha Press Ltd 1987
Text © Oxford Scientific Films 1987
Art Director: Treld Bicknell   Design: Naomi Games
ISBN 0 416 63880 5
10 9 8 7 6 5 4 3 2 1
Printed in Hong Kong by South China Printing Co.

The publishers wish to thank the following for permission to reproduce copyright material: **Oxford Scientific Films Ltd.** for pp. 1, 4, 6, 7, 8, 9 *below*, 11, 12 *both*, 13, 15, 18, 19, 20, 22 *above*, 23, 24, 25 *both*, 27, 29, 31, front and back cover (photographer Peter Parks); pp 2, 3 *below* 9 *above*, 14, 21 and 26 (photographer David Shale); p 16 *above* (photographer G. Merlen); p 16 *below* (photographer Keith Gillett); p 17 (photographer Sean Morris); p 22 *below* (photographer Laurence Gould); p 28.

The line drawings are by Lorna Turpin